The Prestige

Doncaster 3

The Corporation

John Banks

© 2005 Venture Publications Ltd

ISBN 1 905304 03 X

Cover: Doncaster was well known for its fleet of exposed-radiator AECs in the postwar period. On 8th May 1958 No. **135** (**MDT 220**) was photographed wearing the second postwar livery. *(Roger Holmes)*

Rear cover: A move away from AEC saw a number of Leyland Titans enter the Doncaster fleet, all with exposed radiators. Number **191** (**191 NDT**) was a 1963 Titan PD3/4 with Roe 72-seat bodywork, seen here in July 1972 carrying the third postwar livery. *(Roger Holmes)*

Inside front cover: Number **60** (**CDT 34**) was a wartime delivery into the Doncaster fleet, in 1942, and its utility bodywork was by Roe. The single-decker is AEC Regal III No. **23** (**MDT 223**), dating from 1953. *(Both: Roger Holmes)*

Inside rear cover: The Doncaster coat of arms. *(Roger Holmes)*

Title page: In wartime markings of white wing tips and guardrails and masked offside headlamp, AEC Regent No. **58** (**BDT 949**) was brand new and awaiting entry into service in June 1941. This was the classic early-wartime combination of "unfrozen" chassis *(see page 8)* and bodywork to prewar standards. *(Senior Transport Archive)*

Below: Time-served buses converted for breakdown and towing duties were a feature of many municipal fleets and Doncaster's was no exception. **DT 7615**, seen rescuing disabled trolleybus No. **375** at Armthorpe Road/Sandringham Road, was a 1936 Leyland TS7, originally fleet number 5. The Leyland bodywork had 32 seats when the vehicle was in passenger service. *(Roger Holmes)*

>> *Opposite page:* Trolleybus No. **374** (**CDT 626**), a 1945 Roe-rebodied (in 1955) Karrier W, is seen at the Barrel Lane Balby terminus. That location was well known among the youthful conker-playing fraternity and trolleybus crews were frequently pestered to use the bamboo trolley-retrieval pole to knock conkers of the horse chestnut trees, seen in the background of this picture. *(James Firth)*

Introduction

The Local Government reorganisation of the mid nineteen-seventies brought much anguish to students of the municipal road passenger transport scene. To the "war babies" (such as the writer, who emerged into this world in 1942 in Kingston upon Hull to the sound of bombs falling and buildings collapsing around him) and those born in the decades either side of the Second World War, formative years had been spent with familiar vehicles, liveries and routes, and drivers and conductors were recognised figures in the daily round; sometimes, even, they were friends or relations.

The municipal operators, from the tiny fleets such as that of Bedwas and Machen through the medium-sized organisations exemplified by Bournemouth, Hull, Leicester or Portsmouth to the giants at Birmingham, Glasgow, Liverpool or Manchester were each unique: not part of any group, they pursued with smart and efficient vehicles a policy of serving their ratepayers who came to know by heart what ran where and when and used the bus or trolleybus as a matter of course. Even those who owned cars seldom went to work in them for the bus would convey them there cheaper and not much slower - sometimes, if car-parking was a problem at or near work, a good deal quicker.

But nothing is permanent. All is ephemeral. The livery that one grew up with suddenly changed from a dignified and restrained base colour with cream or white stripes and occasionally curves to something quite different, at the very least reversing the proportions of the existing livery but often introducing completely new colours; the familiar, trusted route numbers were prone to be changed, too, in many places for no reason it seemed other than to satisfy some desk-driver's wish for "order"; vehicle suppliers came and went, too often at the whim of an incoming official - who will ever forget the influx of Leyland Titans at Nottingham in 1957 after decades of perfectly satisfactory AEC Regents that had been the major presence in the fleet since 1930? At least in Hull when Leyland Atlanteans appeared after similar reliance for years on AEC Regents, there was the excuse that AEC did not offer a chassis layout suitable for one-man operation. Fares went up, after years of stability, more and more often and in ever-increasing percentages; the friendly conductor disappeared, to be found in the driving cab doing two jobs for not much more than the same wage and with neither time nor inclination for the hitherto regular exchange of pleasantries or even a brief chat. As if all that were not too much fate then brought us the various political and administrative reorganisations that caused many municipal operators to disappear.

Such a one was Doncaster, which ceased to exist after the end of March 1974. Doncaster! What a fleet! What a town for the transport enthusiast!

Apart from the railway interest, with the Plant, the station, the Gresley Pacifics, the Deltics, there were literally dozens of different bus and coach operators' vehicles to be seen. There were long-distance coaches of United and East Yorkshire (among others) as well as the single- and double-deckers - some modern, some rather less so - of the many independents; the company fleets such as those of East Midland and Yorkshire Traction were there; on race days the influx of private-hire coaches was a sight to amaze: and there were the trolleybuses and buses of the Corporation.

From my childhood home in Kingston upon Hull Doncaster was a far distant foreign country never visited for its own sake but passed through several times a year on the way to visit grandparents, uncles and aunts who lived in Nottinghamshire. This passing through was at first accomplished by train from Hull to Doncaster and onward by bus and thus the awestruck infant never managed to escape into the wider purlieus of Doncaster. Then we moved up a peg when along came the family Ford 8, a venerable machine, tiny, shiny, black, reliable and surprisingly nippy, that nevertheless required about three hours for the 70-mile journey. Passing through Doncaster from boundary to boundary revealed trolleybuses at outer termini, motor buses all over the place and that hidden treasure the tree-lined bus stands around Christ Church with all those independents. It was wonderful but the Olympians would never stop and let me out of the car and in any case I had no camera.

There had been trams, although I didn't know that until many years later, from 1902 to 1935. On 2nd June of the former year the Doncaster municipality's first public transport system began with two routes - to Balby and Hexthorpe - and later in the month a route to Bennetthorpe was inaugurated. Bentley and Hyde Park were reached later in 1902.

In the following year a further three services were started, including the Oxford Street route, which was controversial, not a financial success and was suppressed in 1905. The Beckett Road and Avenue Road services of 1903 followed lines of route earlier established by horse-bus operations.

Like many another system Doncaster's offered "spokes of a wheel" routes from the centre of the town out to various points in the suburbs and it was not until 1911 that cross-town services were attempted.

In 1915 the tramway route mileage stood at 11/ miles following the introduction in that year of an extension of the Balby route to Warmsworth and a new route to Woodlands. That same Woodlands route saw the last tram journey on 8th June 1935, although the replacement of the trams by trolleybuses and motor buses had started in 1928.

Motor buses and trolleybuses had first appeared in 1922 and 1928 respectively and by the time I began to know the fleet, in passing so to speak, the trolleybuses were already falling out of favour though not to finally disappear until towards the end of 1963, after I had been to Doncaster on several visits as a camera-toting enthusiast. Alas, my early photographs were total failures and, if I may pre-empt my acknowledgements for help received in the production of this book, I am grateful to the people mentioned in the captions for so splendidly filling the void.

The desire to replace the trams with trolleybuses went back at least to 1925 but officialdom and bureaucracy move ever slowly in such matters and it was August 1928 before the first trolleybus route - to Bentley - was opened. There was a lot of trolleybus activity in the next three years with routes to Hexthorpe and Beckett Road commencing in 1929, circulars to the Race Course and to Hyde Park in 1930 and in 1931 the Wheatley Hills and Balby conversions were opened. That

completed the system that was to remain substantially unaltered (there were some minor extensions) throughout Doncaster's trolleybus operating years.

The Black Boy Hotel to Skellow Road was chosen for the first motor-bus service, which began in October 1922. Rossington and Hatfield were reached later in the year and Edlington early in 1923 and from 1925 expansion was rapid. Single-deckers were used for the 1922/3 inaugurations; double-deckers appeared from 1925.

So much for the services (and this has been, of necessity, a very brief survey): what did the Doncaster Corporation fleet have to offer the enthusiast from out of town? I never knew the trams, though there was a link with my home town in that the trucks, motors and equipment from Doncaster's 1920 batch of ten English Electric/Brill 21E cars are believed to have been sold to Hull following withdrawal in the mid-1930s. The earlier trolleybuses had disappeared, too, before I was in a position to take notice. They had been Garretts and Karrier-Cloughs delivered 1928-31. A series of Karrier E6s bought from 1934 to 1939 survived well into the postwar era. The favoured coachbuilder had been Charles Roe, of Crossgates, Leeds, but in 1944/5 some Karrier W austerity trolleybuses appeared with Park Royal or Brush bodies. Postwar additions to the trolleybus fleet were all second-hand: from Darlington and Southend-on-Sea Corporations, the Mexborough and Swinton Traction Company and Pontypridd Urban District Council. These acquisitions brought BUT and Sunbeam chassis (and some familiar Karrier Ws) into the fleet and further Brush and Park Royal bodywork, as well as examples by East Lancs and Weymann. Many of these acquired trolleybuses were rebodied by Roe, two indeed having been acquired for that purpose as chassis only. The Doncaster fleet included six-wheeled trolleybuses, which were a source of wonder to the writer-as-small-boy, passing through captive within the family Ford, for the home system back in Kingston upon Hull boasted only four-wheeled examples.

When trolleybus operation ceased in the town in late 1963 No. 375 had the sad honour of running the final journeys on 14th December. That vehicle is now preserved at

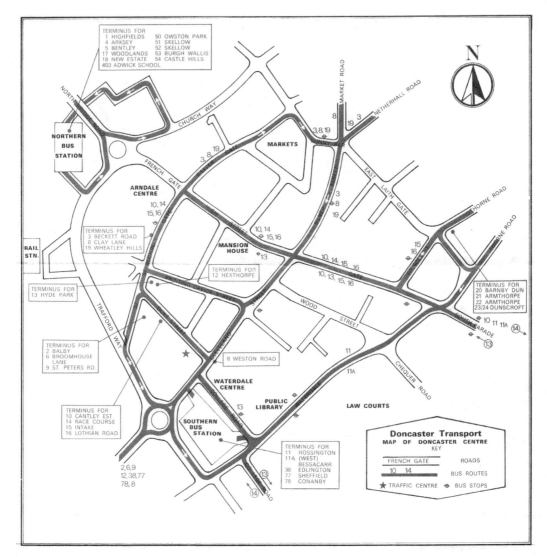

Above: *The central area of the Doncaster municipal transport system in the early 1970s. Tram and trolleybus routes were a thing of the past and soon the operator itself would also be gone. (John Banks Collection)*

Right: *The 1972 Davis corporate livery gave rise to some dismayed scratching of heads among both passengers and enthusiasts (some people were both, of course). Regardless of the impression it made, it was most carefully thought out and a corporate identity manual was issued in June 1972, which laid out in the minutest detail how the scheme was to be applied to the undertaking's vehicles. (Bob Rowe Collection)*

Sandtoft. Many of the Roe bodies were transferred to motor-bus chassis.

Doncaster's motor-bus fleet was never really standardised, although Roe had the majority of the orders for bodywork throughout the operator's existence. Chassis were initially from Bristol and were bought, alongside other makes, for as long as the type was generally available, i.e. up to 1948. In the prewar period, apart from Bristols, chassis from AEC, Daimler, Dennis, Karrier and Leyland were purchased, the most impressive being some six-wheeled Leyland Titanics and AEC Renowns.

The Second World War brought to Doncaster, as it did to most other operators,

problems of vehicle supply. Initial wartime deliveries were of what were termed "unfrozen" chassis. These were vehicles able to be built from stocks of parts that had been in existence at the outbreak of war but whose use had been frozen by ministerial decree, later relaxed. From 1942 for the rest of the war Guy and Daimler austerity chassis arrived in small numbers. Austerity chassis, and their bodies, were built to a somewhat spartan Ministry of Supply specification and the resultant complete vehicles were allocated to operators by the Ministry of War Transport. Operators had to apply for these vehicles and did not necessarily receive what they wanted, or any at all unless a good case had been made out.

Following the restriction placed on Bristol Commercial Vehicles of supplying chassis other than into the state-owned fleets, Doncaster continued to favour AEC as well as investing in Daimler and Leyland chassis. The rear-engined revolution took a while to catch Doncaster in its net and in 1967 the first Daimler Fleetlines arrived. There were never any Leyland Atlanteans.

The last years of the undertaking before its vehicles and garages were transferred to the South Yorkshire Passenger Transport Executive on 1st April 1974 were enlivened under the aegis of General Manager R R Davis MCIT, MITA, AIRTE, who introduced a red livery with a swooping purple stripe lined with white - a livery not universally welcomed among either enthusiasts, who did not matter to the undertaking, or passengers, who ought to have done - as well as having aspirations towards becoming a private-hire coach operator. For the last-mentioned, the Ford chassis was chosen: one came second-hand from a Welsh operator in 1971 and some new Caetano-bodied R1114s were bought in 1972/3. Another new chassis make in those final years was the Seddon, some 42-seat twin-door buses and some small dual-purpose 21-seaters.

The Transport Act, 1968 caused the County of South Yorkshire to become a "passenger transport area" (what had the area been before, one wonders?) It is even today not universally understood what the political and bureaucratic maze spawned by that Act really meant and this is not the place to analyse it. Suffice it to say that there came into being the South Yorkshire Passenger Transport Authority and the South Yorkshire Passenger Transport Executive whose joint remit was "to provide a properly integrated and efficient system of public passenger transport to meet the needs of the areas in question" (was that not what Doncaster Corporation had been doing for several decades?). In pursuing this aim, the Authority laid down the general policy to be followed, and the Executive carried it out.

Doncaster went into the new organisation, but so did the municipalities of Sheffield and Rotherham and with the adoption of a new tan and cream livery all traces of Doncaster's individuality disappeared.

Acknowledgements

This book would not have been possible without the help of Roger Holmes, who has generously provided the bulk of the illustrations, and of Bob Rowe (whose knowledge of Doncaster stems from both enthusiast and professional viewpoints) and Bob Ashton, whose reading and checking of text and captions is gratefully acknowledged. Illustrations have also come from the Senior Transport Archive and from the writer's own collection, which includes the work of Geoff Coxon and G H F Atkins. Mary and Dave Shaw have again read the proofs and Ron Maybray has, as ever, been on hand to sort out vehicle specification and identity details. Thank you all. Renewed thanks, too, to The PSV Circle, whose publication PB2 *Doncaster Corporation Transport* was an invaluable research tool.

John Banks
Romiley, Cheshire
October 2005

Above: The original tram terminus in Station Road. The leading tram of the four in the picture is No. **3**, one of the 1902 ERTCW cars with Brill 21E trucks and 56-seat bodywork.

Below: Number **42**, a 66-seat enclosed English Electric car, was one of the batch of ten of the type delivered in 1920 and of which, it is believed, the trucks, motors and equipment were on withdrawal of the cars in 1933/5 sold to Kingston upon Hull. *(Both: Roger Holmes Collection)*

The first Doncaster trolleybus, No. **1 (DT 821)** was delivered in 1928. It was a three-axle Garrett with Roe 60-seat bodywork. It ran in passenger service until June 1936 when it became the driver-training vehicle, working thus until withdrawal in July 1938. The upper picture gives us a nostalgic view of some attractive and now-disappeared buildings at Doncaster Race Course. *(Senior Transport Archive; Roger Holmes Collection)*

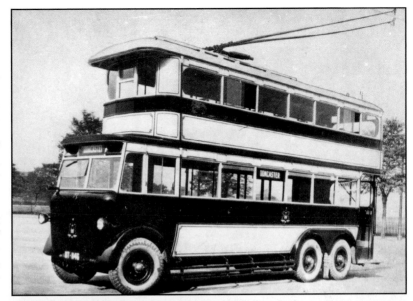

Upper: The 1928 Garretts were a batch of four (fleet numbers 1-4): the remainder of the year's ten trolleybuses (Nos 5-10) were the first of what was to become the Doncaster standard - Karrier-Clough E6 models with Roe 60-seat bodywork. The six of 1928 are typified by No. **8** (**DT 1146**) (*Senior Transport Archive*)

Centre: There were six more standard Karrier-Clough/Roe 60-seaters in 1929 (Nos 11-6) of which No. **14** (**DT 1749**) is shown on 28th July 1931 in a nostalgic traffic scene in St Sepulchre Gate West coming in from Hexthorpe. It was about to enter the loop turning arrangement at the inner terminus. A few days short of two years old, the trolleybus had already had its lower panels, originally cream, repainted. A similar vehicle in the background had just turned out of the loop on the outward run. (*G H F Atkins*)

Lower: A similar batch in 1930 (Nos 17-23) is represented by No. **18** (**DT 2003**) in a busy scene at Hexthorpe Park Gates. (*G H F Atkins*)

Upper: Another of the 1930 machines, No. **20** (**DT 2166**), was photographed leaving the Hexthorpe and Balby services terminal loop, entering St Sepulchre Gate on its way out of the town centre. *(G H F Atkins)*

Centre: Another batch of six standards in 1931 took the fleet numbers to 30; No. 31 was a Bristol demonstrator, formerly a motor bus new in 1929. It was rebuilt as a trolleybus in 1930 and sent to Doncaster Corporation, who purchased it in 1932. A solitary new trolleybus in 1934 was No. **32** (**DT 4718**), a 60-seat Karrier E6 whose Roe bodywork was to a somewhat smoother outline. *(Senior Transport Archive)*

Lower: The Karrier E6 machines in 1935 (Nos 33-9) were further improved in appearance with a refined profile, as demonstrated by No. **37** (**DT 6539**). *(Senior Transport Archive)*

Above: The handsome rear profile of 1935's No. **37** (**DT 6539**) on the Wheatley Hills service near the Wheatley Hotel.

Below: By 1939 the standard Doncaster trolleybus based on the Karrier E6 chassis and Roe 60-seat bodywork was a refined machine. In that year there was a batch of 20, Nos 49-68. Number **52** (**BDT 117**) is seen before entering service. *(Both: Senior Transport Archive)*

The Karriers from the second half of the 1930s were to survive well into the postwar period looking little the worse for the arduous operating conditions of the Second World War. The trolleybuses were renumbered in 1948 and we illustrate Nos **347** and **364** (**ADT 185/BDT 129**) - originally Nos 37/64 - as renumbered and running in the 1950s. Number 347 was at the terminus of the Bentley service on North Bridge and, remarkably, would do a U-turn across what was then the A1 trunk road in order to return to Bentley. Number 364 was in West Laithe Gate. *(D A Jones; D Tate)*

Above: The Karrier/Roe standard six-wheeler to peacetime specification gave way during the war to four-wheelers built to the spartan requirements of the Ministry of Supply. In 1943-5 Doncaster acquired nine Karrier W models with 56-seat austerity bodywork by Brush or Park Royal. **CDT 638** was a 1945 Park Royal example and the last of the nine. It was originally numbered 77 and became **377** in April 1948. It was photographed in West Laithe Gate. *(W J Haynes)*

Below: The wartime Karriers were rebodied by Roe as 62-seaters in the mid 1950s. Number **372** (**CDT 624**) had been a Brush example. It is seen in rebodied form in Thorne Road on 14th September 1957. *(Roger Holmes)*

Above: The postwar Roe double-decker was an attractive design, seen more on motor buses than on trolleybuses. Its rear profile is seen on Doncaster's wartime Karrier W chassis No. **375** (**CDT 636**). It was photographed on 24th February 1963 alongside the depot at Greyfriars Road.

Below: All postwar trolleybus purchases were of second-hand vehicles. The first, in 1952, were six 1949 ex-Darlington Corporation BUT 9611T models with East Lancashire Coachbuilders metal-framed bodies, exemplified in a 24th April 1955 picture at West Laithe Gate by No. **381** (**LHN 783**). These BUT trolleybuses were unique in that Doncaster sold them to Bradford in 1960 and they thus became the only British trolleybuses to serve three undertakings. *(Both: Roger Holmes)*

Above: Nine Sunbeam Ws came from Southend-on-Sea in 1954. The first of them, No. **384** (**BHJ 827**), had a Brush austerity body seating 56, the others had Park Royal bodies. All were later rebodied by Roe. This September 1958 view shows the original body. The vehicle was on Race Special duty and was parked in Catherine Street.

Below: The Mexborough and Swinton Traction Company also supplied Sunbeam Ws: eight in total, of which two were chassis only. Again, all were rebodied by Roe. Number **398** (**EWT 515**), as rebodied, was in West Laithe Gate on 14th June 1958. *(Both: Roger Holmes)*

Above: Motor buses in the first three years of operation, 1922-4, were all Bristol single-deckers, on either the 2-ton or 4-ton chassis as 20- or 30-seaters. Number **12 (WY 2835)** was typical of the 4-ton version, with Bristol two-door bodywork seating 30. It is seen at Rossington when still quite new. *(Roger Holmes Collection)*

Below: The first chassis not from Bristol was No. **51 (WT 9078)**, an AEC 504 type with Roe 50-seat open-staircase bodywork, seen here when brand new. *(Senior Transport Archive)*

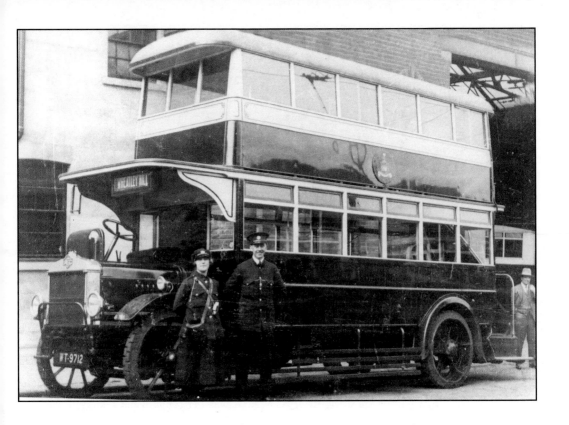

Above: A contemporary of the vehicle in the last picture was No. **50** (**WT 9712**), a similar Roe-bodied 50-seater. Numbers 50/1 were withdrawn in 1930 and sold to a Sheffield dealer.

Below: Roe-bodied AECs also entered the Doncaster fleet as single-deckers in 1925. Number **14** (**WU 484**) was one of a pair of forward-entrance 30-seaters on the Type 503 chassis. WU 484 also had a short life, even by the standards of the time, being withdrawn in 1929 and scrapped in 1931. *(Both: Senior Transport Archive)*

Above: The six AECs bought in 1925 did not immediately convert Doncaster: apart from one ex-demonstrator in 1926 it would be 1934 before the next Doncaster order to the Southall manufacturer. In the meantime, Bristols remained popular, and in 1926 a pair of A-type 50-seat double-deckers (Nos 55/6) bodied by Short Brothers were placed in service of which this one, No. **55** (**WU 9230**), was the first. Another Bristol A, No. 57, was delivered at the same time but was stored and did not enter service until 1928 *(see page 21)*. *(C Carter)*

Below: A Bristol A demonstrator had preceded the two described above. Number **54** (**HU 7236**) is shown after having been rebodied in 1933 with the shortened body from a 1928 Karrier WL6/2. The photograph was taken at the former aircraft hangar depot in Leicester Avenue, which was extended in 1938. It had been intended that trolleybuses would use this depot but such development was stopped by the outbreak of war. *(L Flint)*

Upper: After the Bristol A type came the celebrated Bristol B type single-decker - the "Superbus": the first for Doncaster were four Roe-bodied 32-seaters in 1927. Numbers 24, 23, 25 and 26 were DT 1-4 in that order, and bore the first registration numbers issued against an index mark allocated to the then new Doncaster County Borough. This one is No. **23** (**DT 2**) when brand new. It was put into service in April 1927. (*Roger Holmes Collection*)

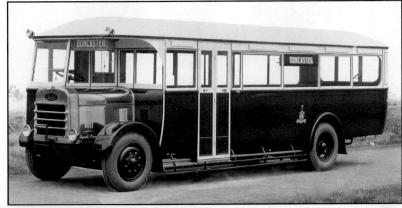

Centre: In another lovely July 1931 street scene from the camera of Geoffrey Atkins, No. **57** (**DT 750**) features in Station Road. Another outside-staircase Bristol A, it was new in 1926 but stored unregistered and not put into service until March 1928. The photographer, whose main interest is the art of the coachbuilder, noted at the time that the body plate acknowledged Bristol, rather than the usually quoted Short Brothers. (*G H F Atkins*)

Lower: Number **63** (**HY 3628**) was a Bristol G-type double-decker, built in late 1931 as a Bristol demonstrator. It was purchased for the Doncaster fleet in 1932. (*Senior Transport Archive*)

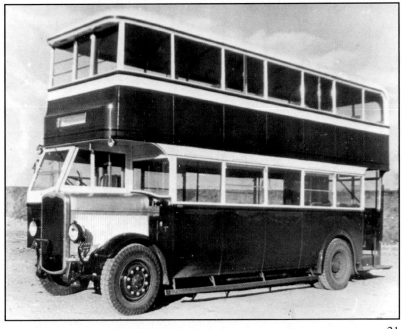

Following the tentative trials of the 1925 AECs the next *marque* to challenge Bristol was Dennis, first seen in the fleet in 1930. In 1931 two fine HV models with Roe 48-seat enclosed-staircase bodywork were purchased. In extremely smart as-built condition was No. **61 (DT 2115)**, the second of the pair. *(Roger Holmes Collection; Senior Transport Arvive)*

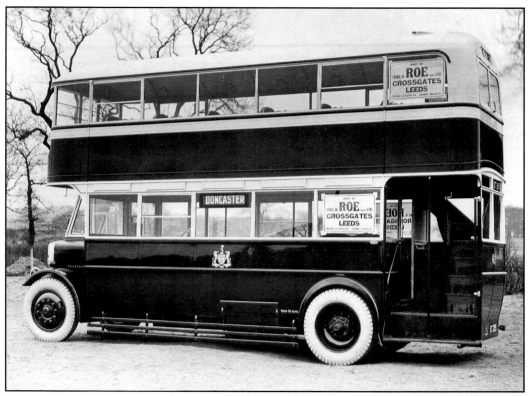

Above: The Bristol "Superbus" on the B-type chassis gained a more modern radiator outline soon after its introduction, as shown on 1928's No. **29** (**DT 669**), a Roe-bodied 32-seater photographed in Sheffield in September 1929. *(G H F Atkins © John Banks Collection)*

Below: The B-type chassis, not long before its demise and replacement by the Bristol J type, again had its radiator shape changed. The new version was to become very familiar on the J, K and L type chassis and in general outline remained unchanged until the end of traditional exposed-radiator buses from Bristol. Number **39** (**DT 3296**) was a 1931 delivery. *(Roger Holmes Collection)*

An interesting and handsome single-decker was ordered for 1933 delivery from Dennis Brothers of Guildford. Number **43** (**DT 4148**) was a Lancet with Roe 32-seat front-entrance bodywork that entered service in February of that year. Although withdrawn by Doncaster as early as 1942, after a short spell of service on loan to Sheffield Corporation, the vehicle went to a new owner, was rebodied and survived until 1955. *(Both: Senior Transport Archive)*

For some observers the glory days in Doncaster began with the mid-thirties six-wheeled double-deckers on Leyland Titanic and AEC Renown chassis. The Renown sold better than did the Titanic but neither type was common outside London (and even there the Titanic was a rarity). Municipalities that did order them - one recalls Bury with its magnificent centre-entrance English Electric-bodied Titanics and the Leicester Renowns - received a lot of bus for the money. Numbers **65 (DT 5276)** and **66 (DT 5337)** were the first examples of each in Doncaster and were new in 1934. Both Roe 60-seaters, they displayed a remarkable difference in modernity of body outline. *(Roger Holmes Collection; John Banks Collection)*

Above: The nearside view of AEC Renown No. **66** (**DT 5337**) points up the awesome size - for those days - of the 60-seat Roe bodywork fitted to the six-wheelers. A small point of interest is that the front-offside wheelnut guard *(see previous page)* was clearly designed to be a driver's step rather than a decorative feature as on the nearside. *(Senior Transport Archive)*

Below: Four more AEC Renowns came in 1935 and then in 1936 three Leyland Titanics. The body styling of the first Titanic had given way to a more modern and smoother profile. Of the three (Nos 71-3) we illustrate No. **72** (**DT 7812**) at Sandringham Road Intake terminus in its first few weeks of service in September 1936. *(G H F Atkins © John Banks Collection)*

Above: Another brand new Leyland Titanic features in this wonderful September 1936 traffic scene outside Doncaster's Gaumont British cinema at the top of Hall Gate. Fleet number **73** (**DT 7813**) gleams in the sunshine as it picks its way through an assortment of other vehicles including a United Automobile Services Tyne-Tees-Thames Leyland Tiger coach. *(G H F Atkins © John Banks Collection)*

Below: The Leyland Titanic in postwar years is represented by No. **73** again, once more outside a cinema, this time the Essoldo in Station Road. The vehicle was still smart, but had lost its polished wheelnut guards. *(C Carter)*

Above: Leyland Motors also supplied single-deckers to Doncaster in 1936: seven TS7 Tigers (Nos 1-7) with, perhaps surprisingly in view of the operator's allegiance to Roe, Leyland's own bodywork. These 32-seaters were converted as ambulances from 1939 to 1945. Five returned to passenger service, including No. **7** (**DT 7617**), seen here in September 1936 when two months old. Withdrawn in 1950, it was converted, using the tower that had been carried by a 1912 Albion and then a 1922 Bristol, for use as Doncaster's tower wagon, lasting thus until 1964. *(G H F Atkins)*

Below: **DT 6903**, which had been fleet number 1, was one of the two 1936 Leyland Tigers that did not re-enter normal service. It did, however, operate as a Doncaster Education Committee school bus from 1945 to 1957. It was photographed on 28th February 1953 outside the Essoldo Theatre now renamed The Grand (at time of writing the object of a preservation campaign) displaying its light green and cream livery. The policy of the Education Department in operating pairs of time-expired Transport Department buses persisted into PTE days. *(Roger Holmes)*

Above: Doncaster's first AEC Regents appeared in 1937 when in August of that year two Roe-bodied 56-seaters (Nos 51/2) appeared. Fitted with AEC 7.7-litre engines, they survived in Doncaster service until the early 1950s. Number **51 (DT 9080)** is illustrated. *(John Banks Collection)*

Below: All these AECs, Leylands and Dennises, as well as a couple of Daimlers in 1932/3, did not dent Doncaster's loyalty to the Bristol *marque* and alongside 1937's AEC Regents there were three Bristol JO5G/Roe 32-seaters (Nos 8-10), exemplified by No. **10 (DT 9084)**. Despite the legendary ruggedness of the Bristol chassis/Gardner diesel engine combination, these three lasted with Doncaster only until 1945/9. *(Senior Transport Archive)*

Above: Although the six-wheeled 60-seat AEC Renown had given way to the four-wheeled 56-seat Regent by 1937, the equivalent switch from Leyland Titanic to Titan did not take place at the same time and in 1938 a further batch of six Titanics (Nos 74-9) appeared, on the TT5c chassis, again with Roe bodywork. Number **79** (**DT 9758**) was the last of the batch and was photographed in Trafford Street after the war. *(Roger Holmes Collection)*

Below: Number **13** (**DT 9761**) was one of three Roe-bodied 32-seat Leyland TS8 Tigers delivered in March 1938. It is seen at Waterdale on 28th June 1952. *(Roger Holmes)*

ADT 887 was the notable Doncaster Committee Coach. Never used, or intended, for public passenger service, it was a luxuriously equipped 16-seat Leyland LZ2 Cheetah. Put into use in early 1939, its Roe body boasted armchairs, settees and a Board Room table. The vehicle was withdrawn in 1954 and scrapped in 1960. *(Both: Senior Transport Archive)*

Above: Nineteen-thirty-nine's public service vehicles included Bristol, Daimler and Leyland chassis, all bodied by Roe. The Bristols were a batch of four 32-seat single-deckers (Nos 14-7) from which No. **14** (**BDT 222**) is shown at Trafford Street on 7th October 1951.

Below: **BDT 222** was withdrawn in December 1956 and transferred to Doncaster Education Committee use in February 1957, lasting thus until December 1961. For this work it carried the fleet identification "**A**". Similar vehicle 224 was "**B**" for like duties. In its green and cream livery BDT 222 was photographed in the depot yard on 30th June 1957. *(Both: Roger Holmes)*

Above: Doncaster had bought two Daimler CP6 chassis in 1932/3 but did not return to the *marque* until 1939, when a single COG5 was acquired and fitted with a Roe 54-seat body. Number **53** (**BDT 226**) is seen in pristine condition when brand new in June 1939. *(Senior Transport Archive)*

Right: Wartime and postwar rebuilding often altered municipal buses considerably but Doncaster's remained relatively original in appearance, as shown by No. **53** in July 1951. The rebuilt windows are the most obvious change. *(James Firth)*

Above: The Leylands in 1939 were three TD5 Titans (Nos 54-6), of which the middle of the three, No. **55** (**BDT 228**), is seen in August 1951 at Trafford Street. *(James Firth)*

Below: A superb portrait of No. **58** (**BDT 949**), one of three AEC Regents delivered in 1941, and seen near the Infirmary in Thorne Road. Two years into the war, the Roe 54-seat bodywork was still to peacetime standards. Wartime utility chassis and bodies were just around the corner, however. *(Roger Holmes)*

Above: Nineteen-forty-one also saw a batch of three Bristol L5G single-deckers, again with Roe bodies to prewar outline, delivered into the Doncaster fleet. These 32-seaters took the fleet numbers 18-20. Number **18** (**BDT 979**) is seen at Glasgow Paddocks bus station on 31st May 1955 on a short working to Conanby of the joint Sheffield service. Of the three operators, Doncaster, Sheffield and Rotherham, only Doncaster worked shorts to Conanby.

Below: These Bristols lasted for two decades in Doncaster service, all three being converted for one-man operation in late 1957, running thus converted until withdrawal in November 1961. Number **20** (**BDT 981**), photographed near Trafford Street on 5th March 1960, wears its years lightly as it shows off the conversion. *(Both: Roger Holmes)*

Above: AEC Regent No. **60** (**CDT 34**) of 1942 had Roe bodywork to the angular outline necessitated by the need to follow the Ministry of Supply's utility specification for wartime buses.

Below: In the same year Doncaster's first utility Guy Arabs were delivered. A total of eight would be acquired in 1942/3, with bodywork variously from Brush, Massey, Roe or Weymann. Number **81** (**CDT 186**) was one of four to carry Massey bodies. *(Both: Senior Transport Archive)*

Above: The 1943 Guy Arabs included three with Roe lowbridge bodies, a seating layout not hitherto represented in the Doncaster fleet. Numbers 84-6 were 55-seaters and we illustrate No. **85** (**CDT 291**) in the depot yard on 30th June 1957. *(Roger Holmes)*

Below: The wartime double-deck-bus building programme also included chassis from Bristol and Daimler and Doncaster was allocated three 1943 Weymann-bodied 56-seat Daimler CWA6 models, of which No. **89** (**CDT 311**) did not enter service until February 1945. *(Senior Transport Archive)*

As always at such times of crisis and emergency the wartime vehicle building programme took some time to be organised and implemented and MOS utility vehicles were still being delivered in 1946 although the war had ended the previous year. Although the Guys and Daimlers of 1942/3 had no doubt been welcome Doncaster, as a major Bristol user, might have hoped for an allocation, which finally came in 1946 when two K6A double-deckers, one each bodied by Strachans and Roe, were delivered. Number **90** (**CDT 677**) was in fact to relaxed utility standards and had upholstered seats from new instead of the wooden slatted variety. It was the last utility-bodied bus to enter the Doncaster fleet and is illustrated twice to show the change (in the 1950s) from the three-cream-bands livery to the simplified single-band version. *(Senior Transport Archive; Roger Holmes)*

Right: The two Bristol K6As in 1946 were accompanied by a Daimler CWA6, which was bodied by Roe to peacetime standards. In this picture No. **91 (DDT 239)** was at Trafford Street on 14th April 1960. It was withdrawn at the end of 1963.

Below: The second of the 1946 Bristol K6As was also bodied to peacetime specification and profile by Roe and No. **92 (DDT 590)** makes an interesting contrast with No. 90 on the previous page. The photograph was taken at Christ Church on 6th October 1962 a matter of weeks before the vehicle's December withdrawal. *(Both: Roger Holmes)*

Above: The first buses to full peacetime specifications and standards of both bodywork and chassis were Leyland-bodied Titan PD2/1s ordered for 1947/8 delivery. The first of them, No. **93** (**EDT 702**), one of two delivered in November 1947, features in a May 1949 photograph at Sandringham Road Intake terminus. *(G H F Atkins © John Banks Collection)*

Below: There were two more all-Leyland PD2/1s in 1948 and all four were rebodied in 1963 with ex-trolleybus Roe-built 62-seat bodies. The second of the 1947 pair, No. **94** (**EDT 703**), is seen after the rebodying, in a scene outside the Gaumont cinema taken nearly three decades after, and forming a fascinating contrast with, the upper picture on page 27. This vehicle survives in preservation. *(Roger Holmes)*

In another comparison of the first and second postwar livery schemes the vehicle is No. **96** (**EDT 705**), the last of the four 1947/8 Leyland PD2/1 Titans. It was photographed when brand new *(above)* and on 15th April 1961. In 1963 it was fitted with a body from a withdrawn trolleybus. *(John Banks Collection; Roger Holmes)*

Above: In addition to the Titans 1948's deliveries included four Bristol K6As and five Daimler CVD6s, all bodied as 56-seaters by Roe. The last of the batch of Bristols, No. **100** (**EDT 793**), was also the last for Doncaster from that manufacturer, which henceforth would be restricted to supplying to the state-owned operators. In a May 1949 picture, the vehicle was at the Intake terminus at Sandringham Road.

Below: The five Daimlers were the first of a batch of 16, completed in 1949. Number **105** (**FDT 828**) was a September 1948 arrival, seen in Station Road, near the Grand Theatre. *(Both: G H F Atkins © John Banks Collection)*

Above: The first five of the 1949 Daimler CVD6/Roe double-deckers were 56-seat highbridge machines that carried on the FDT registration sequence from the 1948 vehicles. Representing Nos 106-10 is No. **107** (**FDT 830**), photographed on 1st May 1965 near Doncaster's railway goods dock.

Below: The Doncaster index mark had changed to GDT by the time the next Daimlers were registered and Nos 111-20, whose delivery ran over into 1950, were GDT 420-9. Typical of the batch was No. **113** (**GDT 422**), seen at Trafford Street on 14th May 1960. *(Both: Roger Holmes)*

In 1951 two eight-feet-wide buses, a Daimler CVD6 and an AEC Regent III were delivered. Both Roe 56-seaters, they had various special features including an air-conditioning system and a double-step to the platform. The extra width over the then 7ft 6ins standard was not found useful in Doncaster and Nos **121/2** (**KDT 392/3**) were withdrawn as early as 1955, the Daimler going to Leon of Finningley and the AEC to another local independent, Blue Ensign. Both were at Sandringham Road, the Daimler in February 1953 and the AEC the following September. *(James Firth; G H F Atkins © John Banks Collection)*

Above: The 1951 eight-feet-wide AEC Regent, No. **122** (**KDT 393**), was sold to G H Ennifer, trading as Blue Ensign, of Doncaster in November 1955, for whom it ran until 1967. It then had a spell as a driver-training vehicle before being acquired for preservation in 1972, being brought back to running order in Doncaster livery by the middle of 1986. In this 2003 view at Sandtoft, it was taking pride of place in a display of ex-Doncaster vehicles.

Below: Doncaster joined in the underfloor-engined revolution in a modest way in September 1951 with No. **21** (**KDT 391**), an AEC Regal IV/Roe centre-entrance 40-seater. In November 1960 it was converted for one-man operation as a 38-seat dual-doorway vehicle. The photograph was taken in May 1965 by the side of Leicester Avenue depot (opened in 1938) and the vehicle was withdrawn in the following October. *(Both: Roger Holmes)*

Above: To add to the variety of the AEC single- and double-deckers and the Daimler in 1951, there were a further two all-Leyland PD2/1 Titans, Nos 123/4, of which No. **124** (**KDT 563**) appears in an October 1961 photograph taken at Trafford Street.

Below: Like the earlier postwar Titans, these two were rebodied using Roe 62-seat ex-trolleybus bodies. Number **123** (**KDT 562**) gleams in the sunlight in this July 1964 picture at Thorne Road taken very soon after the vehicle's re-entry into service. *(Both: Roger Holmes)*

Although Doncaster's could never really be said to have been a standardised fleet, around 1950 it did seem as if the Daimler CVD6 was finding favour. Then in 1951, as we have seen, AEC began to make inroads and no other make was bought between 1953 and 1962. In 1953 there were both single- and double-deckers, the latter typified by AEC Regent III/Roe 56-seater No. **127** (**MDT 227**) at Sandringham Road on the last day of February 1953. *(James Firth)*

Above: The 1953 AEC Regent IIIs with their half-cab, open-platform, 56-seat bodies by Roe were in time to be painted in the earlier livery of dark red with three cream bands and looked extremely smart. They epitomised, indeed, all that was best about traditional municipal bus operation in British towns and cities in that era. Number **127** (**MDT 227**) stands out like a beacon in this traffic scene from early in its life. *(Senior Transport Archive)*

Below: They were just as handsome from the nearside, shown by No. **126** (**MDT 226**) photographed when four months old in another traffic scene at the Gaumont cinema. Vehicles following included a Jeep, a Bedford Model O truck and a new Ford Consul. *(G H F Atkins © John Banks Collection)*

Above: At Glasgow Paddocks on 21st July 1962, No. **128** (**MDT 228**) shows the difference wrought by the newer livery of a lighter shade of red with one cream band.

Below: The AEC single-deckers in 1953 were three Regal IIIs with Roe 39-seat bodywork. Number **22** (**MDT 222**), now preserved, is seen on 8th June 1963. *(Both: Roger Holmes)*

In 1954 there were more AEC Regent IIIs but for 1955 the model specified was the new Mark V version of the Regent; because Doncaster specified a 7ft 6ins width and exposed radiators the difference was not so marked as it was in fleets where wider vehicles with enclosed radiators were specified. The second of many Regent Vs to enter Doncaster service was No. **138** (**TDT 338**), seen here on 14th June 1958 at Duke Street. *(Roger Holmes)*

Above: Disaster befell No. **151** (**XDT 151**), a 1957 AEC Regent V, when it left the road and overturned into a ploughed field between Sprotbrough and High Melton on 12th February 1969, following which it was stripped for spares and scrapped.

Below: In 1958 Doncaster Borough changed to reversed registrations. The first buses so registered were more AEC Regent Vs of the by now familiar style with exposed radiators and built to an overall width of 7ft 6ins. Number **165** (**4165 DT**) is seen in April 1961. *(Both: Roger Holmes)*

Above: Having bought a solitary underfloor-engined chassis in 1951, Doncaster steered clear of the type for a decade and then in 1961 took six AEC Reliance 45-seaters bodied by Roe. Another 1964 traffic scene outside the Gaumont cinema includes No. **30** (**8630 DT**).

Below: AEC lost Doncaster in 1962 when Leylands and Daimlers were ordered, including Daimler CVG6/Roe 62-seater No. **170** (**170 GDT**), seen on its first day of service, 7th July 1962, on the Rossington service, jointly operated with East Midland, Rossie Motors and Blue Ensign. The body was a former trolleybus unit. *(Both: Roger Holmes)*

At the same time as buying chassis constructed to dimensions that would accept the bodies rescued from withdrawn trolleybuses, Doncaster in 1962 started to buy 30ft-long chassis to accept Roe 72-seat bodywork. Both Leyland Titan PD3/4 and Daimler CVG6/30 types were acquired. One of the Leylands, No. **175** (**475 HDT**), is illustrated at Glasgow Paddocks bus station on 8th June 1963. *(Roger Holmes)*

The Daimler CVG6/30 version of the Doncaster 72-seater is represented by No. **178** (**478 HDT**) at Christ Church, again on 8th June 1963. *(Roger Holmes)*

Above: A view from a different angle of a former trolleybus body, 7ft 6ins wide and with 62 seats, as mounted on an early 1960s Daimler CVG6. These bodies had been fully fronted when new in the period 1957-9 and the conversion to halfcab specification for motor-bus use was carried out by the original body manufacturer, Roe. Number **185** (**585 HDT**) was photographed on 13th April 1966. *(Roger Holmes)*

Below: Here is the controversial 1972 livery of all-over red relieved by a purple band edged in white as it was applied to a traditional 72-seat double-decker. Number **174** was registered 474 HDT but here, in a rare mistake by the signwriter, it is **174 HDT**. The picture was taken in Sheffield in February 1974. *(G H F Atkins © John Banks Collection)*

Daimler CVG6 chassis with the narrow former trolleybus bodies are here shown carrying the 1972 livery and also as renumbered under SYPTE (Doncaster District) control. Numbers **1173/84** (**173 GDT** and **584 HDT**) were photographed in 1976. *(Both: Senior Transport Archive)*

The last 7ft 6ins-wide chassis bought specifically to receive ex-trolleybus bodies came in 1963 in the shape of two Leyland PD2/40 Titans, Nos 188-9. The first of them is shown *(above)* in June 1964 and *(below)* in 1977 carrying the 1972 livery and operating as part of the SYPTE driver-training fleet. The vehicle has been preserved. *(Roger Holmes; Geoff Coxon)*

Above: A batch of five Leyland PSUC1/11 Tiger Cubs augmented the underfloor-engined segment of the fleet in 1963. Roe 45-seat bodywork was provided and the batch 31-5 was registered 431-5 MDT. The first of them, No. **31** (**431 MDT**), was photographed outside the Doncaster Corporation depot at Leicester Avenue on 2nd May 1965. *(Roger Holmes)*

Below: Number 33 (**433 MDT**), as renumbered **1033** by the PTE, was in this 1977 view carrying the 1972 livery modified to record the 75th anniversary of public transport in Doncaster. *(Geoff Coxon)*

Above: More maximum-length forward-engined double-deckers came in 1963/4, featuring Roe 72-seat bodywork on either Leyland Titan PD3/4 or Daimler CVG6/30 chassis. Number **194** (**194 NDT**) is seen in original condition in this April 1964 view at the back of French Gate. *(Roger Holmes)*

Below: The Daimler CVG6/30s are represented by what was originally No. 200, here renumbered **1200** by the PTE (**200 NDT**) and photographed in 1974. Alongside was No. **1220** (**DDT 220H**), a 1970 Daimler Fleetline. *(Geoff Coxon)*

Above: The Leyland Royal Tiger Cub was a rarity, built specially for Doncaster, who ordered a batch of ten (Nos 36-45) for 1965 delivery. The chassis were 33ft 6ins long and the Roe dual-doorway bodywork had seating for 45. Number **42** (**FDT 42C**) was photographed on 13th April 1966 against a typical railway-dominated Doncaster backcloth with North Bridge prominent. Ten more Royal Tiger Cubs were delivered in 1968/9. *(Roger Holmes)*

Below: In another livery comparison, the 1972 scheme is seen superimposed on the same vehicle - by then renumbered **1042** - in a 1974 photograph. *(Geoff Coxon)*

Above: The first rear-engined double-deckers, in September 1967, were two 78-seat Daimler Fleetlines, bodied by Roe. The first was No. **208** (**RDT 428F**). *(Senior Transport Archive)*

Below: One of the second batch of Leyland Royal Tiger Cubs of 1968/9, for which the styling of the Roe 45-seat bodywork differed markedly from that of the 1965 batch. The representative member of the class is No. **51** (**UDT 451F**), photographed on 20th May 1973. *(Roger Holmes)*

Above: Seen in a September 1969 photograph, Daimler Fleetline No. **210** (**YDT 210G**), new in May of that year, demonstrates Doncaster's pre-purple-band livery as applied to the rear-engined concept.

Below: In the last four years of its existence, Doncaster turned to Seddon for single-deck service buses including, in 1972, a batch of eleven RU models with Roe 42-seat dual-doorway bodywork. This one, photographed in July 1972 when only a month old, was No. **72** (**MDT 472K**). *(Both: Roger Holmes)*

Above: In pursuance of the undertaking's attempts to become a coach operator various vehicles were acquired in 1970-3, starting with No. **20** (**CDT 420H**), a Willowbrook-bodied Ford R192 service bus that was fitted with 45 coach seats before entering Doncaster service in March 1970.

Below: A Ford R226 was acquired second-hand from Bebb of Llantwit Fardre in 1971. The 53-seat coachwork was by Duple. *(Both: Roger Holmes)*

Above: Added to the coach fleet in 1972 was No. **19** (**LDT 119K**), a Caetano-bodied Ford R1114 53-seater, seen here in May 1973 on private hire work. *(Roger Holmes)*

Below: Among the last vehicles bought by Doncaster were some small Seddon Pennine 4-236 models with dual-purpose 25-seat bodywork also by Seddon. Originally No. 22, by now renumbered **1022** in the PTE fleet, **TDT 622L** was working the Inner Circle in 1974, only a short time after the formation of the South Yorkshire Passenger Transport Executive. In recalling the Titanics, Renowns, Regents, Titans and Daimler CVD6s, and comparing them with the Fords and Seddons of the last days of the undertaking, we might perhaps take our leave of one of the smaller, but not less interesting, of the municipal public transport undertakings that proudly served their people for so many decades. *(Geoff Coxon)*